Spiked with Laughter

Spiked with laughter and laced with life, these wise and witty verses are for those who seek humor in casual events, in the absurdities and contradictions of the social swirl . . .

Poems with personality, rhymes with reason—call them what you will—they run a wide gamut of topics touching on myriad interests, from golf to grog, from cats to capers. Seasoned as spice and politely sophisticated—they are most of all funny in a lightly happy and human way.

Sincere regards to

Gary Bickford

Manley Reece

Spiked with Laughter

by

J. D. Manley Treece

Illustrated by Morris Martindale

Binford & Mort

Thomas Binford, Publisher

2536 S. E. Eleventh • Portland, Oregon 97242
1974

Dedicated to all those good friends and loyal relatives who were kind enough to think that these verses have some merit.

Proem to a Poem

The verses contained herein are the result of an effort to accomplish an improvement in memory, especially the memory of personal names. Tradition has it that the ancient bards of Scotland not only developed prodigious memories but verbally recorded history by memorizing long epic poems. Encouraged by this precept, the writer memorized and then wrote poetic doggerel based on events and circumstances as they occurred.

We are greatly indebted to Mrs. Gordon Manary for timely advice and counsel and to my wife Ann for her co-operation and willingness to be the subject of several verses.

The reader may find the results humorous and, in some cases, they may even contain bits of acceptable facetious philosophy.

> *So:* As you follow these verses through,
> Perhaps you'll find a friend or two.
> But ere you put them on the shelf
> Read on and you may find yourself!

J. D. Manley Treece

Contents

The Memory Plan

It all began with a memory plan
To bring me local acclaim,
A foolish man who hopes he can
Learn to remember a name.

So I memorized up to my eyes,
Stanzas and verses galore.
They couldn't deny I gave it a try
'Til I couldn't absorb any more.

So now my mind though quite refined
Has failed to bring me the fame.
It's simply uncanny how I fall on my fanny
When I try to remember a name!

Genius at Work

My life is replete with tasks incomplete;
With dreams of the deeds that I plan.
Like writing a book or catching a crook
Or finding a Savior for Man.

It's my firm intention to make an invention
Surpassing all those gone before.
But, while we're debating these dreams I'm creating,
Let's fill up our glasses once more.

Nothing New

For centuries on end the writers distend
Their thoughts on life's great stage.
Ideas replete, with rhymes complete,
On events of every age.

Ofttimes we find a similar kind
Of philosophy or of themes.
They duplicate, at times inflate,
Poetic romantic dreams.

And thus it shows one rarely knows
A surpassing way to convey it.
It's utterly true, there's nothing new
Except in the way you say it!

In a Self-Made Man-er

The trouble with a self-made man
Be he Doctor, Merchant or Baker—
He wastes an awful lot of time
Praising his modest maker.

T'anks a Lot

Dear Husband: Now I'm leaving you
And I've taken the Coupe Deville.
I'm eloping with that haughty man
From the station over the hill.

If at times I have regrets,
And life is not all clover,
Always will I keep in mind
That my tank shall runneth over.

And should this man run out of gas
He'll no longer be my swain.
That's the day with an empty tank
I'll come back home again.

Try a Fry Out

The Indian said of the Mermaid,
As she went swimming by,
"Not enough girl to make love to
And not enough fish to fry!"

The Only Way to Fly

A gauge of futility is to test the ability
Of man with his fabulous brain,
To corner a fly, as he goes winging by,
While buzzing his utter disdain.

For man with his science, has placed his reliance
On methods which none can defy.
But the fly keeps on flying, without hardly trying
'Cause this fact is unknown to the fly.

Adam and Leaves

For countless eons the leaves have fallen
From all the plants that had 'em.
Of all those millions the important one
Was the leaf that fell for Adam!

The Weigh-in

That gracious one who runs my house,
A thoughtful, kindly, wonderful spouse,
Is careful that she won't get "round"
And peruses closely every pound.

Like a training athlete she has her "weigh-in"
To hold the poundage she would stay in.
All jewels and watches she curtails
As she slowly creeps up on the scales.

One hand on the rail, careful and slow,
She tries it lightly with a dainty toe.
Then, boldly she makes the final stroke,
Steps on the scales and "goes for broke."

The needle moves to its destined place.
She greets the news with sad grimace,
Observes the pounds with abject sorrow,
Then swears she'll diet—starting tomorrow!

Medicinal Only

Did you ever stop to ponder
Why the game is eighteen holes—
Why not twelve or twenty
With the flags upon the poles?

Those shrewd discerning Scotsmen,
Who oft played in chill and rain,
Depended on Scotch whiskey
Their ardor to sustain.

They found a fifth of whiskey,
When divided into drinks,
Would ward off chill and ague
While touring on the links.

One ounce and a half of the medicine,
When swallowed eighteen times,
Kept them warm and healthy
In those rigorous Scottish climes.

Eighteen drinks and the fifth was empty—
That determined the length of the fray.
So eighteen holes was decided
As the perfect number to play.

Double Trouble

It's not my intent to e'er disparage
That institution known as marriage.
All weddings are filled with happiness double—
It's living together that causes the trouble.

Show and Tell

A human recorder we have at home,
A four-year-old who hears it all,
Records it in his little dome
And discomfits us by full recall.
Repeats it in exact detail,
No neighbors or friends excluded,
No phrase or clause does he curtail,
With expletives included!

Hells Bells

The devilish job of catching souls
Is Satan's occupation.
How come he does so very well
From such a poor location?

A Bar-grin

Put a smile upon your face
The way that Nature meant—
It brings you friends, it gives you grace,
And it doesn't cost a cent.

The Eyes Have It

If lots of sleep will make you well—
Keep those circles from under your eyes.
How come we always look like hell
In the morning when we arise?

Difficult

Hiding behind a woman's skirt
Was once considered tragic.
The skirts they're wearing nowadays
'Twould call for a bit of magic!

Devaluation

Now they've devalued the dollar.
Now they've devalued the yen.
Now they've devalued the reichsmark,
And they may do it all over again.

The thing that concerns me severely,
And I hope they will some day explore,
Is a method to follow quite clearly
And devalue my golfing score.

London — England

Wrong Number

Now it's patriotic to share your bath 'n tub,
Conserve the heat and water and help each other scrub.
It sounds a whole lot better than the baths we took alone
But while we're swapping soap suds, who the hell will
answer the phone?

Battle of the Bulge

Why is it called middle age
When the seams begin to burst?
I guess it's called middle age
'Cause that's where it shows up first.

Comic Stripping

Do you wonder what the world will be
Two hundred years away?
Science, discoveries—the things we'll see
At that far-off distant day?

The wonders of that day sublime,
Today's great ones eclipse,
But we shall know ahead of time
By reading the comic strips.

The Good Map

Unfold the roadmap—scan the pages,
Then comes the mystery of the ages,
How to fold it back again
The way it was when you began.

Let's Face It

We have a new book at our place,
Which tells you how to save your face.
You squint, you grin, you stretch and yawn
And hopefully all those lines are gone.

So now at our evening cocktail hour
With vodka, gin or whiskey sour,
We pass the time, just me and Mother,
Making faces at each other.

Patriots All

Now we're conserving energy
And you may serve your country well
When you lower the heat and dim the lights
In the places where you dwell.

We're getting closer together,
Not because of personal charm.
We're getting closer together
Just to keep each other warm.

So snuggling up is the thing to do,
For reasons non-erotic.
With the heat turned down you "bill and coo"
And it's strictly patriotic.

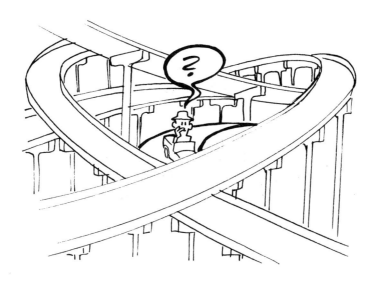

Uncle Ben

Remember those tales of yesteryear
When people were prone to disappear,
Leaving families sore distraught
Knowing not what fate had wrought?

The modern version of that story
Left our family sad and sorry.
It happened to our Uncle Ben,
And well do I remember when.

Down the freeway he was cruising
Exit signs with care perusing.
He missed his turn—did Uncle Ben
And we never heard from him again.

Well Seasoned

When several years or more go by
And a friend seems out of season,
Then suddenly he looks you up—
Be sure you know the reason.

Corny I Guess

At cocktail parties we inhabit
They talk of aches and ills,
Of accidents and operations,
Of exotic cures and pills.

Each person has his favorite tale.
He tells it o'er and o'er.
The listeners all are spellbound
While the boaster holds the floor.

They count their stitches one by one,
Relate the marvelous cure,
Tell of pacers on their hearts,
And the corrections they endure.

So I'm at a disadvantage
When I tell *my* tale of woe,
For folks don't seem to give a damn
About the corn upon my toe!

Fa'ther On

They now have a day for Father
When the Old Man's on display—
He spends it blithely paying bills
Left over from Mother's Day.

It's All Behind

We went on vacation to forget it all
And put annoyance out of mind.
We planned that we could have a ball
And just leave everything behind.

We packed those boxes, grips and crates,
Supplies of every kind.
We drove away; forgot our freight,
And left every damn thing behind.

The Numbers Game

The "fifth" is a famous number,
Be it either amendment or flask,
It adjusts to all sorts of uses
Brought on by the aim of the task.

The amendment we take to keep silent,
Thus leaving some facts unsung.
The flask with its contents so potent
Works mostly to loosen our tongue.

Timely Thirst

I received an invitation
To a cocktail rendezvous.
It contained a stipulation
That festivities would ensue.
Time was of the essence—
They put it somewhat tersely
That they expect my presence
Promptly at six "thirsty."

Druthers of Others

Experience is based upon mistakes,
But could I have my "druthers,"
I'd base my knowledge on mistakes
Already made by others!

Physics

The shortest route between two pints
Is defined as a true straight line.
For some that line may waver
Drinking whiskey, beer or wine.

So don't be fooled by science.
That line is hard to follow—
Especially if you tread that line
With legs that may be. hollow.

Trust Not

'Most everyone is honest—
That's why I think it's funny
You can't trust any son-of-a-gun
With your sweetheart or your money!

Ever So Clever

The Lord in his wisdom, as we grow old,
Dims the sight in our eyes.
The various things that we behold
Assume a different guise.

So, as in the mirror, we view our face
His subtle plan is clever.
To our ancient eyes we still have grace
And we look just as good as ever.

A Foul by an Owl

The stately Owl, wise and astute,
Spends hours in contemplation—
Waiting for his time to hoot
And preserve his reputation.

With solemn orb and baleful eye
He awaits his proper clue—
To put to voice his lonely cry
With a mournful resounding "Who!"

Wise he may be, but still we wonder,
And maybe we're right to assume
That the wise old Owl has made a blunder
Said "Who" when he should have said "Whom."

The Worldly Wise

Intelligence, wherever found,
Is a virtue nonpareil.
Though rare, it need not e'er astound,
When it proffers its learned spell.

So easy for me to recognize,
This quality we rarely see.
The ones who are so worldly wise
Are the ones who agree with me!

Lemon Aid

My wife is raising lemons
On our penthouse patio,
To supplement our diet
And to save a little dough.

My spouse is fond of lemons;
She has a yellow thumb.
We find it very pleasant
When combined with gin or rum.

So now I know the reason
And can readily foresee,
If she's that fond of lemons—
That's why she's fond of me!

The First Shall Be Last

A lesson we learned in days of yore,
And still in our minds may loom,
Ofttimes the man who opens the door
Is the last to enter the room.

Whatever Is Left Is Right

Now they have left-handed checks
Designed for those undeft.
The stub is on the right-hand end
Where it once was on the left.

We can't see that it matters much
To the awkward or the deft.
The important thing we'd like to know,
Is there any money left?

I Knew Him Well

When an old, old friend by chance you meet
In the lobby, the shop, or out on the street—
He greets you as neighbor, old buddy, good friend
Or other names of a similar trend.
Don't be too flattered by his hearty acclaim—
It's likely he just can't remember your name.

Intense Intent

They say the Arabs fold their tents
And softly steal away;
Disappear into the night,
To return another day.

The modern camper works his damnedest,
While his temper bile ferments,
Trying to figure out just how
Those Arabs fold their tents.

Relatively Speaking

When finally it comes your time to go
Be heartened by your fate,
For that's the time for pomp and show
And review of your estate!

Noah Foolin'

When opportunity meets preparation—
That's the time when luck abounds.
So plan ahead with calculation
On safe and solid grounds.

Prepare yourself ahead of time.
Be ready to make your mark.
Remember it wasn't raining
When Noah built the Ark.

Personal Pot

Nowadays we hear an awful lot
About that "grass"—sometimes called "pot."
Our generation doesn't need to try it.
The pot we have is cured by diet.

Thighs and Size

We note that fashion now decrees
That milady expose her thighs and knees.
Garments intended for covered flattery
Now expose much more anatomy.
And so we observe so very sadly
That most need covering—Oh! so badly!

The Scots Have It

No one in the world should ever scoff
At those canny Scots who invented golf.
They play so well, from the day they start,
We try like hell—never master the art.
When they viewed our swings and the shots we botch
That's when those rascals invented Scotch!

Green Thumb

The "green thumb" set now has a claim
That plants need conversation.
That sweet talk with the proper aim
Breeds faster propagation.

They speak to greens in dulcet tones
Be they aster, rose or daisy;
When comes that day the blooms speak back
We'll know that someone's crazy.

Respectfully Yours

Treat your friends with great respect.
In kindness there's no danger.
Mark you well, except for them,
You'd be a total stranger.

Stocks on the Rocks

We've explored the Moon and Mercury too.
Science is moving apace.
There's nothing the human mind can't do
In this world or out in space.

What puzzles me and many more,
And deals us daily shocks,
Is why they can't invent a lore
To predict those wavering stocks.

Question Hour

Somewhere, somehow they changed my clock
And left me sad and sour.
This question gives me quite a shock—
"Did I gain or lose an hour?"

One by Three

They say that one of every three
Is mentally unsound.
I wonder if it's thee or me
Who's risky having 'round?

So check with care your two best friends.
Should you find them both well spun—
This is where the story ends
'Cause you must be the one.

Two Alone

In the Garden of Eden, just Adam and Eve,
Destined to live there and never to leave—
Still Eve said to Adam, "Do you love only me?"
And Adam replied, "Who else could it be?"

Flirting License

Sometimes at parties with our wives,
Their watchful eyes remind us,
Of fishing on an ample stream
With the warden right behind us.

Save Your Breath

Two things I claim are good advice
And both I will defend,
Never run up a stairway
And never run down a friend.

Antiques at Home

My loved one possesses and constantly seeks
Gold-plated teapots and exotic antiques,
Tables most ancient, saucers and mugs—
Our household's resplendent with crackleware jugs.

It's obvious she favors the old not the new.
Things that are useful she strives to eschew.
As time marches on and I pass my peak
She'll rightfully place me with those other antiques.

Too Tight

If you're burdened with weight on your mind,
And a ready solution wish to find,
By your pride be not misled—
Just take that "halo" off your head.

Irish Ire

The ideals we built in childhood
Historians now erode.
Columbus, alas, was third in line
When on our shores he strode.
Bacon, they say, wrote Shakespeare's plays.
Washington liked his wine.
Blackstone's laws were not his own.
Lincoln was unrefined.

But now there comes the hardest blow,
A pretention low and vile.
They're claiming that noble St. Patrick
Ne'er came from the Emerald Isle.
They say they never had those snakes
On Hibernia's sacred soil.
The Irish only saw those snakes
While imbibing that homemade oil.

We Irish hang our heads in shame,
As we down another beaker.
If St. Patrick isn't Irish
Then Santa Claus is a streaker!

"Woodn't" You Know

The way we cut and waste that stuff,
And burn it if you please,
You could suspect that we might think
That lumber grows on trees!

Silence Is Golden

When we are in our infancy,
The days of dreams and fantasy,
It takes two years to learn to speak,
To run and shout, and loudly shriek.

When finally we reach maturity,
And find we need security,
We start a plan of verbal diet
Learning the virtue of being quiet!

Up a Tree

An amorous Tomcat climbed up a tree
To seek out his lady love—
He thought that she might possibly be
A pigeon or a dove.

A storm blew up, Old Tom crashed down—
That's when he spoke these words,
"Making love up in the trees
Is strictly for the birds."

Economics

Capital and Labor, a symbolic pair,
Need explaining with prudent care.
Capital is that possessed by others—
Labor is getting it away from those brothers.

Czar Car

A dictator model is my arrogant car—
A tyrant on wheels, a mechanical czar.
It buzzes, commands, if my seatbelt's unfastened.
If the key's not in place I'm promptly chastened.

If lights are not proper or brakes unreleased
It snarls at me quickly like some angry beast.
If I speed o'er the limit it screeches and wails
Evading the stigma of some local jails.

But strange to relate I'm used to this scene.
I've had the same treatment with different routine.
Once 'twas my wife who ruled knobs and switches—
Now 'tis my dashboard that leers, sneers and bitches!

Neither a Lender Be

'Tis better far to give than to lend
To a relative or a so-called friend.
No wasted time on futile claim
And the eventual cost is much the same.

Free Thinker

Now I believe in the aphorism
That truth shall set me free.
I kept it in my catechism
But little did I foresee,
When to my boss I spoke the truth
It seemed to arouse a quirk.
Freedom was my lot, forsooth,
I was immediately out of work.

Sitting Pretty

Hard, straight chairs and lectures long
Combine to prove for sure,
That the human mind can just absorb
What the tailbone can endure.

Home Life

As I enter into my domicile,
When the hard day's work is o'er,
She greets me with a kiss and smile,
Just inside the door.

A martini is ready, mixed with care.
My slippers and jacket await.
Like a paragon I'm welcomed there
By my thoughtful, sweet little mate.

Just then a light starts shining thru,
As I wrinkle my jaded brow,
I slowly quaff that soothing brew
And wonder what she's up to now!

Has she wrecked the car or bought a dress?
Are relatives coming to call?
Is there something else she might confess?
So I might know it all?

Has she been arrested for speeding?
Has her license been reversed?
Two more drinks I'm needing
Then I shall hear the worst!

"Birden"

For years the stork has taken blame
For births that have occurred;
When often that filial claim to fame
Belongs to some other bird!

It Can't Be Perfect!

Now that women's liberation
Is spread across the entire nation
And the women must do everything alone—
They may ration their caresses
But who the hell will zip their dresses
When the womenfolk are strictly on their own?

Girl Talk

Dear Abby oft quotes sage advice
For girls when boys pre-empt.
"Mind your manners, firm but nice.
Familiarity breeds attempt."

A Trait Ungreat

Why are people all so prone
To cherish troubles not their own,
To delight in stories of those others
And repeat misfortunes of our brothers?

Why could we not in silence stand
And then perhaps to understand—
Forbearance is a virtue true
Which works for them as it might for you?

Time Capsule

Time is the thing so very ample
That puts a stop to vice.
When a man's too old to set a bad example
He starts giving good advice.

Bannister of Life

The bannister of life is a downhill slide
Which sooner or later we all must ride.
Here's hoping that when it comes your day
The splinters are pointing the other way.

Return to Sender

I sent a gem to the publisher;
To me it was really the one.
Like some of my checks
It came back marked "insufficient fun"!

Cheetah or Cheater

A Cheetah pursuing an ungulate
Destined for lunch or snacks
Found himself in a hell of a state
As he flipped upon his back.

That's when he coined that famous phrase
Addressed to all his kin
"I bring you all this sad dispraise—
That *Cheetahs never win.*"

First and Last

Profit or money—let's make it first—
Assuage our hunger, need and thirst.
And may we wisely then forecast
To make it first—then make it *last*!

Island That Is

Two New York Indians opened a bar,
Their coffers so to fatten.
They set a price of 24 bucks
For one little old Manhattan.

Ali-money

He failed to pay the alimony
The judge assessed against him.
That's why he ended up back home—
His wife had repossessed him.

Doggerel

Plants and trees embarrass me.
Their names I can't recall.
Maple, Fir or Cottonwood—
I seem to forget them all.

But Dogwood trees are something else,
When I find one in the park.
I always know a Dogwood tree
By its distinctive canine bark.

The Master Plan

Lives there a man with soul so dead,
Who never once has turned his head,
To view a "lovely" go flaunting past
And dream that dream by instinct cast.

No man shall harbor such a soul,
It matters not how high his goal,
For nature molds in the master plan
A bit of tomcat in every man!

It's Always Possible

Courtship is that wondrous time
Of gift and flower and letter,
While a lovesick girl makes up her mind
If somehow she couldn't do better.

Sounds Fishy

The Mermaid turned up pregnant,
And explained with a knowing nod,
"It never should have come about—
It must be an act of Cod!"

At Wit's End

Once there was an amateur
Dispensing rhyme and wit.
He soon found out the important thing
Was knowing when to quit.